Mirrors Made of Ink

Shannon Quist

Word Noodle Press

MIRRORS MADE OF INK

Acknowledgements

"My Real Mom" was previously published on Anne Heffron's blog August 23, 2021.

Lead cover concept artist: Emery Simmons
Cover designer and illustrator: Theodore Underhill

ISBN

979-8-218-39640-4 *Paperback*

979-8-218-39639-8 *Kindle Ebook*

To Emery and Aunt Bev, we were always meant to have each other.

In loving memory of Carole Anne.

Table of Contents

Foreword

"I see more of myself in ink than I do in the mirror."
- Andromeda Moon

There is no coherent beginning or ending to my story. This particular tale spans several lifetimes and it won't end with me, but still, it's time to document some things. At the very least, there can be a beginning and ending to this chapter.

As an introduction to this collection, I'd like to present you with a consideration of how we change over time and how, with our regrets and anxieties, our histories and our hopes, we flit about from the present to the past and future almost constantly. The poems included in this book follow a thoughtful arc of the actual timeline of my life events, but the vast majority of pieces were written in the past five years or so.

The passage of time has been a strange experience for me. Or rather, the way I feel it progress has never been quite right. I sometimes feel as though I float through and every once in a while, when I take the time to look at myself in the mirror, everything is different from the last time I took stock. Did you ever hear the story of the boy who had a magic ball that could fast forward the passage of time? It's called "The Magic Thread" and a version of the folk tale was printed in *The*

Book of Virtues. The Adam Sandler movie, *Click*, is based on that story, too.

The difference is that, unlike the complete amnesia that Peter (from the story) and Michael (from the movie) experience, I can vaguely remember the dark periods if I try hard enough. Writing helps. It forces my memory to track the ways in which I do and don't recognize myself as I grow. It's also a way to preserve those memories, like fossils in the sediment. The feminist anthropologist Sherry B. Ortner once said that, as a construct of culture and how the patriarchy defines gender roles, "woman's body seems to doom her to mere reproduction of life; the male, on the other hand, ... creates relatively lasting, eternal, transcendent objects, while the woman creates only perishables--human beings" (14). But I intend to contribute to the world and live on in both ways: through the creative artifacts I leave behind, and in the heart of the little one that follows me.

It's important that I hold onto these moments of awakening to jot down a hasty word photograph of my experiences; it's the only time I feel fully alive, and even if the photographs aren't of the same time my physical body occupies, they're still worth recording.

In that spirit, a more technical explanation of the composition time required for this collection is now due. Barring one special exception, the earliest poem in this collection is from 2009. The most recent is from 2023. In that time span, a lot has happened, but the basic gist is that I became an adult adoptee in 2009, began my tentative search for my first mother nine years later, and said my final goodbye to her in 2023.

This is a wordy scrapbook of some of the moments I have recorded in the only mirror that seems to reflect accurately: words on the page. I'd like to share this collection of that ink as it pertains to my experience with adoption, and yes, you can expect a few splotches.

Click. Directed by Frank Coraci, performance by Adam Sandler, Sony Pictures Entertainment, 2006.

"The Magic Thread." *The Book of Virtues: A Treasury of Great Moral Stories*, edited by William J. Bennett, Simon and Schuster, 1993, 57-63.

Ortner, Sherry B. "Is Female to Male as Nature is to Culture?" *Feminist Studies*, vol. 1, no. 2, 1972, pp. 5-31.

The First Letter

A twin bed with new sheets, new carpet, the smell of just-finished drywall, fresh paint, wallpaper glue. This is my new bedroom, built so the three of us, me, my sister, and now my brother, will have our own rooms. This is the result of my mother's first and only pregnancy.

Sitting on the bed, atop a stiff comforter that hasn't yet been slept with enough to feel right, my parents read a letter to me, their faces grave.

I don't yet know that I'll hide the blood of my first period on the sheets of this bed, too ashamed of my body's existence to tell anyone. Or that I'll tear up the walls of my closet when I sleep there after the privilege of having a bedroom door is taken away from me. Or that I'll make the ugly transition from ignorance to knowing in this space.

For now, the room is a bright new beginning, but my parents are only just getting started in their explanations. And tonight, they're beginning with a letter from a woman whose name I'm not familiar with.

I do not connect the dots like they expect me to.
I do not understand that this woman who's written to me
is my own flesh and blood.

The way they read it, with significance and fear, I can
almost hear the distant call from someone who loves me,
but I don't understand who.

"Do you have any questions?" they ask.
"Who is this from?" I ask.
"Your birthmother," they say.
"You know that God loves you very much, that your
birthmother made the right choice and gave you a better
life."

And when they turn out the lights and leave me in this
cold empty room taking the letter with them, I wonder
about pregnant bellies, joy and fear, the static of
photographs, a woman who wrote me a letter, the
downwards curve of my mother's lips as she read
someone else's words to me, and why I feel so lost. Why?

A twin bed with new sheets, new carpet, the smell of
just-finished drywall, fresh paint, wallpaper glue. This is
my new bedroom, but all I can think is that I hate it.

Mexican?

Her name was Shannon, just like me. Blonde and blue-eyed, she was one of my first dolls, the one that sits at the edge of my memory in front of the others.

It bothers me, this image. Sitting on the floor with a doll named after me who looked nothing like me.

Why did I have a doll that looked like her?

I have other memory reels from much later when I was in elementary. Trying to rationalize it, the explanation.

People told my mom I looked like her and when they did, she beamed with pride. I was close enough, I guess. Not if you looked closely, though. I've always known there was something different from the comments.

"You tan so well," and "Your hair is just so thick." Proof that I wasn't the same. If I was, then I'd look like that Shannon doll, blonde and blue eyed like my dad. Or maybe even brown hair, but definitely the eyes. "Those big brown eyes."

Later I would find the barely filled out sheet about another man, a mystery, who helped inform that mystical code of my genetics.

"Mexican? Catholic? Drinks or did at the time."

And every once in a while, I'd hear a murmur about the "Hispanics." But not to me or about me.

Legally, I'm Caucasian, but my birth certificate is less of a hospital record, more of a legally curated and paid for document made to recreate my identity, my destiny.

But there's something missing that makes me different. And I knew it when I named that blonde and blue-eyed doll Shannon.

Infinity

I used to draw backbones full of sideways 8 signs all
collapsing one on top of the other.
It was the first thing I'd ever drawn that gave me joy.
Just a weird frenzy of loop the loops as they fell down the
page in rippling waterfalls,
like a spine that went on and on
without a body to hold it back.
I hated the ending; the finality of Forever was always
sloppy—
How can you end such
a beautiful thing?
But the doodles all ended, of course,

on an awkward curve

after so many
Forevers.

Birthday Luck

born in mystery, shrouded story,
are you not a piece of myth?
hero with a thousand faces,
where on earth does your soul fit?

on this day, you must keep silent,
lest your good fortune run out.
celebrate in secret, oneness,
faith in mystery, have no doubt.

special though you are, I wonder,
what place you appeared from then,
when you made your mark here on earth,
when you made an entrance, friend.

do not wonder what the joy is
of a story too well known
for in your mystery and unknowing,
you have joy that's all your own.

Mom Space

I would catch her at it during dinner,
fork poised over her plate with some forgotten bite,
a gaze that was rapt yet absent, lips barely parted.
It was the first time I recognized Thought from the
outside inward.
"Mom?" I'd ask, drawing her back from somewhere.
"Oh," she'd snap to, then smile sheepishly. "Just Mom
Space again."
But what did she see there?
I'll never know.
Though every once in awhile, when I was older,

I recognized something deeply sad about her gaze out
the window;
Mom Space wasn't somewhere I wanted to be.

Joe Imaginary

I wish he would come visit me again, Joe.
He was a friend like Tom Sawyer, good-natured trouble,
reminding me to look for buried treasure
and be a kid.

Messy hair, overalls, baseball cap.
Barefeet, loud laugh, short like me.
The perfect friend,
even if he was imaginary.

I buried him deep when everything changed.
At the time, I had a sense that I was
probably being made fun of,
but it didn't matter.

When I found out about the schizophrenia,
I felt sick to my stomach. Joe wasn't scary.
He was what I needed when I needed it.
He wasn't so goddamn serious.

So I kept my mouth shut. I didn't want
them to think I was crazy, too.
And now he's just a memory, a ghost I conjured then,
but no more.

Black Nails Bastard

I remember the first time
I heard the word.

Bastard.

Young me, not sure who I was,
wheat fields, preacher man
telling us about hell.
A's in school and youth group after,
but something,
a seed was planted.

Secrets are not good for
small towns.

I remember feeling confused,
little facts in front of me on
worn pieces of notebook paper
folded envelope size,
and that word the next day.

Little miss perfect life,
crumbling under black fingernails.

Stupid little girl who knew
how to find the definition
in the dictionary and apply it.

But the dictionary didn't
explain connotation so
the teacher took her into
the hall to explain.

It didn't get any clearer
after that.

All it taught me was shame
over something out of
my control.

To My Ghost Mother

It was a tomb, that room.
I entered naive, but questions loomed,
impending doom.
Somehow, without a mirror there,
I reflected dark despair while plucking, plucking out my
hair.

It was all mine, that time.
I came out wise, but traumatized,
and half alive.
Somehow, without you next to me,
I saw you clearly in my dreams and pleaded, pleaded,
stay with me.

I'm not your mirror

The pinks of my palms,
and the feel of my hair,
Napoleon stature,
& brown skin when bare,
carcinogen freckles,
skins tags with no names.
Because I look different,
I'm easy to blame.
When whitewashed and painted,
I pass as your dream,
but underneath that,
I'm more than I seem.
The paperwork's empty,
The lawyers left blanks
in the spaces where once,
I had a first name.
You can dress me all up,
you can tell yourself lies,
but these pink palms &
fake docs make me want to die.

Eraser Burn

She touches it sometimes, the one on the top of my left wrist.

I was all of thirteen.
Before the eraser, it was thumbtacks; I'd press them into my skin as far as I could, then watch the little droplets of blood bubble out. Or I'd scrape patterns into my skin until they turned red. Initials, symbols.

But the eraser burn was something different. It's the only one that's still noticeable. The rest have faded away or you have to know where to look, but not this one. This is my forever reminder that once, I wanted to disappear so badly, I tried to erase myself.

I was distraught that my parents still didn't understand me and kept sending me to counselor after counselor. I remember rubbing the eraser over the same spot over and over again until it bled, then sneaking into the kitchen to shake salt on it.

This is pain, I told myself. *You control it. Control the pain. But goddamnit, to control it, you have to feel it.* And I kept at it diligently until the eraser was soaked in blood.

And it never healed. It's still there.

Someday, I'll have to tell my daughter what it felt like to feel worthless, to feel unheard, to have hated myself so much that I wanted to see myself bleed, make myself cry. Someday, I'll have to share my sadness with her in hopes that she never feels the same way.

But for now, she touches it and says, "I have a scar, too. It's on my knee. I fell off my scooter, and it bled so much. Wanna see?"

Run

What they believe about a better life,
an idyllic life,
doesn't have to be what you believe.
Your life was scripted without your consent.
When your parents talk to their friends,
their friends know more about you and your history
than you do.

Your teachers know.
Your doctors know.
That lady who visits with the toys and the clipboard
definitely knows.

They thought that fear tactics would work.
Or distractions. Or reroutes.
Or talks about how great you already have it.

Are you grateful, yet?

They're watching you. They think they can control you.
They think you're beautiful, but it's sick the way they
frame you
in an album you didn't want to be in.

They'll punish you until you conform. Are you going to
take it?

You deserve the truth.

Scream until you get it. Scream until you get the fucking
truth.
It's your story, don't let them write another goddamn
word.

You have to escape.

You have to escape before they capitalize on that bullshit
Hallmark crap
that completely ignores what really happened.

Run.

Little Ballerina

Little ballerina, spin and turn and dance away.
Keep your smile, keep dancing,
make me smile until I say.
I'll wind you up and keep the happy smile upon your
face,
but when you stop, the music's gone, it all begins to fade.

What keeps you here, just dancing?
Do you love to feel this way?
Or is it lonesome in my box, inside your tiny cage?
You can't work on your own unless I wind you up to play,
and when you do, I force the smile that's frozen on your
face.

I feel that way, sometimes, painted, winded up to play.
When nothing works, the music stops, I just call it a day.

Words

Since words are all they taught me,
this is how I speak.
I cannot seem to self contain
these thoughts inside of me.
But words are all I know of
to let myself be known.
And though I am much deeper,
this is how I'm shown.
These words are all they taught me,
I can't seem to get through,
the way I feel about this,
the thoughts I have of you.
And words are all I have now,
though little it may be.
But words are what define this
of whoever I may be.

Can you feel it, too?

Unexpectedly, it comes. I can never predict these moments,
and as soon as I recognize them, my world shifts.
Consciousness or something like it
wobbles around unsteadily as the feeling overcomes my senses.

Me. It's me. Where have I been?

Dancing lazily through awake times when I haven't really been awake,
eyes open, but only two of them.

All the questions I've memorized come crashing through again: What am I? Where am I? How is it that I exist in this particular form? Where did I come from? Where will I go?

I have never had the answers, and I never will, but that doesn't stop the questions from coming. I'll ask the reaper when he comes but by then, it will be too late.

Moments that I've memorized, moments like these come flying out of my memory:

A white suburban, riding shotgun, turning to the east off a loop road.

A dark night on a brick fence, crawling out to anywhere but here.

The principal's office, unblinking brown eyes looking into mine.

A bedroom, perched in a bed that is simultaneously towering towards the ceiling and sinking with gravity towards the floor.

And then, the moment is gone. The crashes always surprise me. What am I supposed to do now?

Even without answers, I must live my life a moment at a time. Catch my breath, return to the strange coincidence of life that, for the most part, I've claimed as mine.

Safe in the Dark

My room, a surprise addition to the house, is close to the kitchen, a place where I can hear her voice, my name. I sit next to the door. I have to know.

I won't move until they go to bed. I can count the times the water runs in their bathroom from the sounds next to my closet. I know how many minutes to wait until they're asleep.

Tonight is the same as always. Still a thrill.

I move quietly through the house, listen for the deep breaths from behind closed doors.

You have to push in the lock on the doorknob of the garage door so it doesn't squeak, and after the initial creak of the first twist, you should pause to listen, then pull the door 45 degrees open fast and finesse the same speed closing it once you're out; it needs to be quick so the hinges don't creak, but gentle so you don't slam the door. One more door to the backyard, the worst door of all, the one you lock behind you. Just in case.

But then you're free.

Safe in the wide open world of after dark.

I am safer strolling down the yellow middle line of the highway than I am in my own house. I am safer hiding from the police; they've only caught me and brought me home once.

I can scream here.

I can be real here.

It's safe in the dark. Even alone.

But the people here are better, too. I've never met more real people than I have after midnight, people who tell the truth, who let their guards down, who feel things, who are so fucking alive.

But it's only for a while, you always have to say goodbye, you know. Everything ends. You have to go back and face it or, at the very least, bear it.

I know the number of minutes it will take me to get home, the time I have to leave, the time I have to be back at. I know when he wakes up, how long it takes him in the bathroom, how long he sits in the kitchen eating Cheerios and reading. When he closes the front door, I wait until I hear his car start before I fall asleep.

I only have an hour before she wakes up.

And then it starts all over.

Speak

My mom's language is music and she uses the piano to
speak.
My dad's language is math and he uses numbers to
speak.
And, just to be generous,
My birthmom's language was drugs, but I don't know if
she ever learned to speak.
And I'm just some weird math equation science
experiment mix of those variants.
And yet something all my own.
Because this is my language. I use poems to speak.

Stereotypical Adoptee Barbie

Hi! I'm Stereotypical Adoptee Barbie. When you think of an adoptee, my situation is what you think of.

I was rescued by an upstanding white heterosexual Christian couple from homelessness, drug addiction, brown people, and misdiagnosed mental illnesses. Wait...

You'd think I feel lucky. But I don't. Here's a list of fun facts about me:

1. My ethnicity was kept a secret, even from the government.
2. Nobody took the responsibility to let me know that addiction ran in my genes.
3. I wasn't allowed to know my biological mother's full name and all correspondence was monitored and censored.
4. I was sold at birth for $20K.

Stereotypical Adoptee Barbie includes existentialism, depression, anxiety, and a tendency towards self harm. Not included: therapy, stability, or a balanced sense of self. Buyer beware: Stereotypical Adoptee Barbie malfunctions violently when put in abandonment situations.

There's Nobody Here But Me

There's nobody here but me.
Why does the air around me reverberate with such violent vibrations?
I'll forever be falling into forever, rippled moments in time, wobbly consciousness.
And what is the point of naming, identifying, labeling, if there is no meaning anywhere?
We'll forever be circling in and out of being, snapshot moments on the page, always just out of context.
Why should you understand me when you don't understand yourself? How can any of us understand anything?
I'll forever be drifting throughout eternity, blinking away the moods of temporary moments; nothing lasts except for me.
Am I doomed to exist like this, forever?

It's Poison

Most of what makes it to the paper.
Most of what I dream.
Most of what you know about me.

I have to spit it out,
coax it out,
dig it out,
Whatever it takes to rid myself of it.

I am nothing so pretty anymore.
These scars of mine hide what I was.
And my confessions never save me.

I don't mean to spit bitter,
But watch out, it's poison.

Bloody Fingernails

A sliver in the sky, like her majesty's fingernail
beginning to rip apart time and space, she's tinged red
tonight, bloody Armageddon waiting to unfold.

But for now, she waits.
And so I wait, too.

She thinks she can hide behind the clouds as they drift
across the sky in fragrant little melodies that sound like
sad guitars whispering.

But I know she's watching me.
And I watch her, too.

My own fingernails scratch restlessly against suntanned
summer thighs, and I remind myself that it isn't the sun
who makes me whole.

But I don't dig in just yet.
And neither does she.

I am less water than I should be, and though this place
was once home, I am further from her pull than ever.

I am not so fluid here; she can't move me.
Or maybe she refuses.

But from one bloody fingernail to another, we nod to
each other, broken pieces of forgotten rock that move
best in the night.

She hasn't abandoned me yet.
But the bloodbath is inevitable.

Forgive me.

Two Strangers

Little yellow blanket around me, I am one day old. In the photograph, she's wearing a blue floral print gown, not issued by the hospital, but packed in her bag ahead of time for when the big moment would arrive. My eyes are closed, tiny fingers curled below my chin. The perm of the 80s, bangs and all, persists atop her head though the year is 1991—

How warm it must have been in her arms, how safe and right, though surely her unsteady breaths made me nervous. I didn't yet know why. But it was an important era for Texas adoptions. I was one of the special cases—half open, half closed. And for me, just another thing to add to my Methodist resume.

It's hard to tell what she would have looked like in person. The picture is a bit grainy, paid for and printed at a Kodak shop downtown. But if you really look, beyond the baby swaddled in yellow, past the posed smile, there is a fear in her eyes, just a flicker—she's about to hand me over to two strangers forever.

She can't know—

That these people will keep secrets about her from me, that I'll take years to gain the courage to seek her out, that I'll believe, like the people who raised me, that I don't have to be like her as if she is something innately wrong. Or that I'll spend years trying and failing to "see the bright side," of the "better life." So many years will pass from this moment to one where I'll follow some of her footsteps, or another one when I come to peace with the tragedy.

All she knows is that two nice, but strange, people have come for me, and they want a picture of us in front of the gaudy framed painting of flowers on the wall.

Caught in Orbit

My world is ending and the earth twirls on,
Cool science, guided by the laws of eons.
But here, my world is but a tiny speck
To the grandiose scheme of what comes next.
What *does* come next? I know, I wait,
The earth slowly spinning day by day.
She's cool, collected, bound by orbit,
Perhaps she knows her fate? But how could she know it?
But me, I know it and I dread the explosion,
It's what comes after long long years of corrosion.
Maybe I should twirl on, let it all pass by,
But knowledge brings fear and so I just cry.

Chameleon

Where do all the chameleons sit?
I haven't met another one yet;
just lizards who want a say in how I blend in with them.

But either way, underneath these rainbow scales, I'm just
a cold-blooded reptile.
Doesn't my identification boil down to matters of heart
and reproduction anyway?

That's all you know of me,
my colors, my blood, my sex.

But you know nothing of my masks and why I wear
them.

Las palabras

Like the catastrophic cry of the crickets resounding, the universe closes in on me.

Time, like the bouncing rubber band of callous calls of frogs bounding back and forth, whips me around in circles.

The darkness is my light.

And I will myself to crawl deeper, shine brighter.

I have not forgotten what it is to be without peace, an animal always at war with the world.

Fight and flight, feathers and fangs, the adrenaline flows like a river, ragged and choppy.

This is how I survive.

It is never quiet, always bloody, an eternity of both cheating death and coaxing it nearer.

But like the crying wind, I will never stop moving, even as the darkness closes in.

Lonely Is

Lonely, thy name is a self in the Is,

detached, forgotten, apart, alone.

Multiplicities elude you.

Without the silver silk of a mirror,

you cannot even exist as your own self.

The Is doesn't care about you.

Oh, Lonely, you are a speck of dark

in a sea of eternal inky blackness.

Take a deep breath, there's nothing to fear.

Lonely, thy name is a self in the Is.

To Be My Mother

You don't have to be motherly to be my mother.
Or pretty. Or rich. Or anything.
You are mine and I am yours because
that's just how it is.

I don't care what they say about you. Once,
you and I were a package deal. I know
because once, my daughter & I were the same.
Maybe you remember the cord cutting.
All I know is that the shock of it has
reverberated with me throughout the years.

The stories are all twisted.
Nobody ever thought to tell me that
what I felt for you when I missed you,
when I read your letters so much the paper thinned,
was love and it was allowed.

I'm allowed to love you.

That doesn't mean I'm not scared. But
being scared is the best time to be brave.
So I'm going to finally say it out loud.

I deserve to hug the body I came from,
and you deserve to know I'm okay.
I'm allowed to honor you as my mother.

You don't have to be motherly to be my mother.
Or pretty. Or rich. Or anything.
You are mine and I am yours because
that's just how it is.

I don't care what they say about you.
I'm allowed to love you.

My Heart

Is two halves that open and shut
like that prayer I prayed as a child:
Open and shut them, open and shut them.
Or maybe like the blood of a mother,
sticky and heavy until I can carry the water no longer,
then a downpour. Always a half moon.
You have to expect the jaws to clamp shut.
My love is fierce and I've been told it hurts.
You're in or you're out,
I'm open or shut.

Leaf Burn

I burned a leaf with my cigarette,
pressed the tip of the fire right into the middle,
left the heart of that leaf changed.

It may have been crunchy and dead already, but the
center burned for a moment,
and the smoke circled around the hole while the hole
grew bigger.
It stopped eventually.
But not before that leaf was left with a scar right in the
middle
proclaiming to all who saw it of the hurt it had been
through.

Makes me think there are some things that never heal.
There are hurts in everyone's pasts that begin to make us
who we are.
That leaf is still a leaf but it will never be the same.

Makes me think about life and hurt and why.
I'm glad to be alive but sad that some things just have to
be that way.
Hurtful I mean.

I Am The Weather

I am a tornado.

I am a hurricane.

I am a soft breeze.

And I am quiet breaths.

No matter my tempo, no matter my intensity, the air around me stirs as I stir.

Blowing up the dirt to excavate the bones.

Striking the sea and puncturing its wholeness.

Comforting those who seek the quiet.

Reminding myself that power doesn't have to mean angry.

And also that power is something mysterious, an abstract art that begs interpretation, much like the wind around us.

But I am not under the thumb of this weather.

I am the weather.

I am the gusts of change that blow through this place.

Tree Psychosis

There's no other word for it than psychosis. I was pushed beyond my limits and something deep within me broke. Let us not talk about full grown trees with entire root systems being ripped out of the ground by a killer tornado, though; I was a sapling with no roots at all, just a stick in the ground trying to figure out how to drink. There was only so far that I could bend backwards, and so, I snapped.

Only I know what I was made for, but back then, I didn't even know that. What would a sapling know of its place in the world if it had grown in infertile soil in the dark? This is why I look so different. I had to go underground, shape-shift, survive against all odds, tunnel my way out and learn how to grow in a different way. I was always going to bloom, no matter who tried to hold me back.

But I am not a tree. I am a god. And my power is change.

I Am Made Of Stardust

Conjured. I am made of stardust.
By some unexplainable burst of energy, the universe
came into being or maybe it was always something in
some form.

And I'm not anything apart from that, the moment of my
entrance some fantastic moment of bright and wild new
life too, though nobody remembers it. Or maybe I've
always been here.

Constructed. I am made of stardust.
By some miracle of science, the universe went through
the trouble of constructing molecular life that would
evolve into the genetic composition that makes up me.

I'm not some dusty piece of ash, though.
More like red-hot combustibles lying in wait for the
right weather, the right time to burn out in an explosive
moment of glory.
Or something like that.

Created. I am made of stardust.

By some stretch of the imagination, you might say that the universe conspired in some way to bring all this life about. "God" or whatever you call it.

But I don't need a creator story to reassure me of my lineage; I was not created by anything but biological parts moving together, a new speck of consciousness pulled into this form of existence.

I am creation itself. Or something like that.

I am made of stardust.

My Real Mom

You know which one I mean.

She is soft, but doesn't come off that way at first, hiding instead behind strong words and a puzzled frown.

She has loved me always, though there have been times when she hasn't known me at all.

She is everything I am, everything I want to be, yet it feels as though I never please her.

Spontaneous, sometimes she buys me spur of the moment gifts, trinkets she thinks might help me climb out of my moods.

Other times, though, she reminds me to grit my teeth and make due with the bare minimum.

She is the only one I can rely on, I'm sure you know what I mean.

She was there when I was born, though she didn't know what would happen to me.

And she was there as I learned to speak, learned to fail, learned to hide.

She didn't always call herself mom, though, nor mother or mama. Not any of the titles you'd think she'd call herself, not for a while at least.

It wasn't until she named the failings of all those women that came before her who said they loved her but fell short somehow of that promise.

And we women, why is it that we are set up for these
failures, taught that our worth revolves around our
families even as our families are hindered from being
what we want them to be?
You know what I mean.
But she didn't let this stop her from loving me.
I love my real mom because she is me.

Beautiful Daughters

"Those big brown eyes," my mom would tell me when she re-lived the moment I was finally legally hers to take home.

"Her hair is so thick," she would agree with the hairdresser when it was time for me to get a haircut.

"You tan so well," she would tell me in the summers when I would turn so dark I didn't look like I belonged.

And yet, our hair and height were similar enough that every once in a while, someone would say to her, "she looks so much like you," and my mom would beam. It wasn't until I was older that I understood my brownness and her whiteness, the colored gap between us.

But with my own daughter, things are different. Even though I know they're present, I don't focus on our physical resemblances so much; instead I love to witness the moments her personality shines through.

"So curious," I tell her when she asks about something she wants to know more about.

"Her soul is so kind," I agree with her teachers when they tell me about their interactions with her in class.

"Your style is uniquely your own," I tell her when she puts together an outfit to wear.

And yet, our physical features are so strikingly similar in so many ways, I often get compliments on how much she looks like me. It won't be until she's older that we'll know what kind of unique gifts and traits of hers will emerge.

But what I'm most proud of are the ways in which our conversations are different. Born to me, yes, but more importantly, a soul all her own to discover as she grows.

It's 3AM, I must be dying

Oh, if I could have one wish, let it be that I'd be allowed to stretch 3AM into eternity, the deepest, darkest, and most quiet time of night, laid out in hours, years, eons.

But please, I want to be rid of that song forever because I am lonely no more.

Tell me you love me, the good parts, that you have accepted that I am a flawed human, and give me one last hug, blood of my blood, my little one. Can you love me even after we part? Did I love you well? Will you be brave and go on without me?

You can, you know. I'll always be with you, but when the time comes, I hope it's 3AM with you beside me.

For My Family

I was born into it, and so were you,
The swirls of different kinds of love.

Mine was first defined by a name whispered, then a new
one signed and changed. I love the stories of names, the
way our parents bless us with titles that fit us just right.

And those names tie us to the ones we love, but I've
never had enough room to write down all the names I've
collected over the years.

It's easy to think that family is a thing defined by
bloodlines and last names and christmases, but really,
our family members escape easy definition.

They're the people that bear you, the ones who raise you,
the friends who keep you, the in-laws that feed you, the
people you're stuck with, and the ones you pick, all of
them choosing forever to love you.

No matter what. And those loves make us whole.

Baggage

We all like to think of our baggage as one big black vector weight, with the label "one ton" on it, like in the cartoons.

And for a long time, I dragged mine behind me, moving ever so slowly, the weight holding me down.

Honestly, how I ever managed to carry it around by myself is a feat that still baffles me to this day, but

the way we think of our baggage shouldn't be that big black ton. We should remember what it really looks like.

It looks like bravery, a hero's shiny gold medal on your chest, the moment you decide to let somebody help you lift it,

And awards and honors for all the people after that until finally you reach a point where you've got a whole baseball team just helping you carry in the groceries, a couple light bags per person, a happy village doing their small part.

You carry some of theirs in, they carry some of yours in, and it all goes in the same pantry where nobody keeps count.

Because even the word "baggage" implies weight in bags, not in tons. And when you have that team, the medal on your chest won from humility,

you're going to be alright.

$0.95, a bargain of secrets

What a deal. Just cancel the subscription later. A big green button above tiny disclaimers.

But. What about the mystery? The freedom of true choice?

Well. I have paper evidence. And after all, it's so cheap, and I'll only look. Nothing wrong with looking, right? Mystery? Curiosity?

The wonderful thing about a mystery is that it doesn't have to be solved. It could be, but it doesn't have to be, nor sometimes can it be. Mysteries are what make the universe beautiful. Our brains fill in the empty spaces where vocabulary doesn't exist yet with what we know—shapes, stories, explanations.

"The moon was like this awesome, romantic, mysterious thing, hanging up there in the sky where you could never reach it, no matter how much you wanted to."

There's just something that changes. The beauty can never be enjoyed the same way again. And if I am the mystery, what does that say about me and how I love myself?

But then again, curiosity gets me high.

Click. Type. It's done, I'm in. Remember to cancel this damn subscription.

Oh god. Look at all this.

Why are the addresses so old? Why does she move
around so much? I thought she was older. That's her
middle initial. That's her dad, two brothers, a sister?
Not online at all. Dad has an email. Two addresses that
probably aren't current. Maybe Dad's? But he's almost
dead. He's 89. Maybe he's still kicking. His house seems
nice.

I can't afford a visit.

Not financially. Not emotionally. Why am I even
thinking this?

My therapist echoes in my head,

You want connection, you want explanation, but remember,
you are you.

You are you. You are you. You are you.

I am me. I am me. I am me.

Nobody can define me.

Only I can define me.

What have I done?

Oh.

What have I done?

"The Series Has Landed." *Futurama*, created by Matt Groening, season 1, episode
2, Fox Broadcasting Company, 4 April 1999.

Back to the beginning

Babcock road, San Antonio. To my right is a behavioral health center called Nix, to my left, a Planned Parenthood. Oh yes, the landmarks are accurate so far.

This is my pilgrimage. A quick hello, irreverent but curious. I want to put my hand on the building where I was born. Or rather the home my birthmother resided while I was growing like a weed in a foreign belly. The first place I existed. In some form.

Hospitals and specialist offices line the road, office buildings in a medical center.
This road feels like Amarillo, but I can't place where exactly. Little pieces of so much Texas inspire so much deja vu, similar cities, people.

I'm nervous to see the place, sure, but I'm also annoyed with the 5:00 traffic. My timing is always impeccable.

There it is, renamed on the brick entrance, but otherwise still painfully 1990s. Goats wander across the street from a little Methodist town.

When I drive in, I see a map naming the different buildings. Dorm. Oasis Center. Horticulture. Cafeteria. Chapel. Garden full of life next to the street, and a chapel next to the main building.

It's closed so I don't get to wander around inside, tell my story.
But I peer in the window.
Paintings of Jesus hang above white couches on top of white tile except the white is yellowed with age, there are cracks in the tile, and the tan brown brick makes all the buildings look tired.
How long has this little oasis been here?
Reminds me of church camp, structurally unsound but full of spirit and people who sway with the music but not with their beliefs.

Get back in my car. I did it; I touched the place.

Time to hit the road.

I would have taken you

For the first time ever, she was on the other side of the phone. I had found her. My aunt.

"My mother called me," she said. "After she found out." My own mother hadn't been returning her sister's letters. She had gone missing. Even their mother, estranged from their family, knew something was wrong. And somehow she found out about it, after the fact.

My mother got pregnant. She went away to stay in the Methodist Mission home. My grandfather probably had something to do with it. He was the one who called her schizophrenic, he was the one who couldn't let go of the hatreds he bred, especially for my queer grandmother, and that affected all four of his children.

So by the time my grandmother found out about it, I was gone. I'd already been sent off to the panhandle of Texas, papers signed, parental rights relinquished. Nobody asked if there was family that would take me, they wouldn't have gotten their money that way. It was too late. The lord's work was done and a white lady got her prayers answered.

When my grandmother called her with this news, the news that the baby my mother called Rose was gone, my aunt slid down the wall holding the phone cord and sobbed. She and my grandmother cried on the phone together. I had been lost.

"I would have taken you," she said to me. I could hear thirty-year-old tears well up in her throat. She had said this before, but not to me. And now, my grandmother is lost, and so much else, lost to me as well. What did any of us gain from this? Even the white lady suffered.

"I would have taken you," she repeated. And together, we cried as both family and strangers together over the phone the first time we ever talked.

Belly Button

Contemplating my navel,
but it's apples to oranges,
your existence and mine.

Thinking about reality,
but it's fiction and fantasy,
the parts that built me.

How can absence define so much?
So I fill it with fluff and stuff.
Don't you?

Limo Ride

In the dream, my aunt and I are walking down the
sidewalk on our way to see my mother.

I worry aloud. My words float around my head like a
storm cloud.

Then we turn the corner, and there she is, leaning out of
a limo window, her hair beautiful, her eyes shining. She's
a younger, brighter version of herself, the biggest grin
I've ever seen.

"Meet ya there!" she hollers, waving at us and blowing
kisses.

We wave back as the light turns green and she
disappears down the street.

"It isn't like that anymore," my aunt says to me, brushing
away the clouds. "She's excited to see you. She's cleaned
her room and everything."

When I wake up, the clash between my hopeful dream
and bleak reality is the first thing I notice.

I hug my pillow tight and squeeze my eyes closed again,
but it's no use.

The dream is over.

Birthmark

They say birthmarks are death marks from a past life,
but that would make this hole a birthmark and a scar,
a scar from the cord cutting, a fatal wound reverberating
between my separate existences.

They say that we won't feel a thing,
but I know better.

How can I be so defined by this hole?
So, I think of myself as a leaf with a cigarette burn in the
middle of it,
empty and beautiful, a time portal between two lives,
both infinite.

I am only half of what I could have been.

Static Change

I am not who I once was.
This is incredible; I have known some to be static
etchings of self, unchanging, immovable.
Please, let me find you to have changed as well.
I cannot take more complacency.

I am who I have always been.
This is incredible; I have known some whose very core
essence has been written over and lost.
Please, let me show you that my strength has always
been here inside me.
I cannot take more of this lying down.

I am a static monument of pain.
The picture of my strength grows clearer as I move.

Will you change?
Will you remain?
And what of you will?
It matters.

Betty Jean at the Bar

A mythology professor, a psychiatrist, a naturalist, and a poet walk into a bar. They chat about heroes and their journeys, the imaginary royal families children daydream about when they wish to escape the families they find themselves in, the mysteries both in our heads and at the bottom of the globe, and the hauntings we endure.

The bartender, Betty Jean, pours all of them into one large bottle and calls the concoction the Ghost Kingdom. The adoptees say it's a magic potion because when you drink it, you are embarking on a mythical quest to discover the true nature of reality, humanity, and your own elusive self. The potion gives you the courage to gaze into the emptiness, past and future. The bar is not real, but that doesn't make the drink (or the trip) any less true.

Campbell, Joseph. *The Hero with a Thousand Faces.* New World Library, 2008.

Eiseley, Loren. *The Unexpected Universe.* Harcourt Brace & Company, 1964.

Freud, Sigmund. "Family Romances." *The Standard Edition of the Complete Psychological Works of Sigmund Freud,* edited by James Strachey. Macmillan, 1964, pp. 235-242.

Levin, Matt. "Isaac Bashevis Singer from Beyond the Grave" *The Paris Review,* 18 Mar. 2019. https://www.theparisreview.org/blog/2019/03/18/isaac-bashevis-singer-from-beyond-the-grave/

Lifton, Betty Jean. *Journey of the Adopted Self: A Quest for Wholeness.* Basic Books, 1994.

Spotted Moon

and crows cawing,
rusted leaves and autumn yawning.
It's been many moons since then,
the bitter nights the cold crept in.
I can feel you past the trees,
a broken spirit, on your knees.
And though I've sent you many prayers,
The hope is empty, naked, bare.
Will you feel me in this veil?
Or is this one more sad dark tale?
Chilly blue sky, bloody leaves,
It's time to migrate, come with me.

Chasing Pieces

I can still do it, you know. I can release the burdens, though it grows harder the older I grow. I was once so lighthearted and now, I struggle to find those pockets of peace I once had in abundance.

I collect the pieces of them as I go along, try to squeeze the sponge of memory out onto the paper in splatters as they will. My life is disordered and so any record of it will be the same.

Sometimes it is like the purging of poison that takes me to other realms. Realms that someday I will finally inhabit for that last eternal moment between life and death, true freedom. To feel it pure, you have to eat it all and wait for your body to reject the rest, however violently.

Other times, it is the still of the night when nobody expects anything from me that I take breath in the cold and I feel my stomach settle, my shoulders fall loose.

It's like joy, impossible to make last, fleeting and triumphant, but nothing can make it stay, nothing can capture it in vision or language to do it justice.

Like joy, I find pieces of peace scattered across a chaotic life, often just out of reach.

But maybe, over time, if I am careful of the jar, these pieces might add up to something someday. Perhaps she can scatter them about like ashes when these pieces of life are all that's left of me.

Madeline & 23

In the dream, our code names were Madeline and 23. By some stroke of luck and detective work, I had found her: my mentor's first ever mentee.

23 invited me to her house, a place full of boxy twists and turns and stairs. We reminisced over some of the assignments both of us had completed under our mentor. Her research was hanging on the walls on the stairways leading up to her work room and mine I pulled out of a folder that I'd brought with me for the occasion.

Once we were hidden away in the attic, she confessed to me that she hadn't finished the job, wasn't strong enough to do the work, and so the relationship had been severed.

"But you know why, Madeline. I can tell you because you understand."

She pulled out a handful of envelopes and a butter knife. The first, she slit open and pulled out a card. Inside, in rainbow letters that had been cut from a magazine and then glitter glued over, the letter read:

You know that I love you, mija. Mi corazon is broken porque you never write back. But I love you still.

23 started to cry. I understood that she couldn't open these letters alone.

"I never looked back," she explained to me. "I never cared to know what possibilities were out there in the universe that never was."

"We can open the rest, if you want," I said gently and put my hand on the crook of her arm. She nodded. But in the distance, we heard a door open and close, and she jumped.

"Next time, Madeline," she said. "My husband's home."

And after I'd escaped through the back door, I wondered why it is that some of us hunt out those impossible possibilities and some of us run from them.

I ran all the way home.

If you're empty

First, take to water, raise the sails, and wander til you
die.
The sea can only go so far until it turns to sky.
That terra incognita at the bottom of the globe
is not a continent of ghosts; there lies your temporal
lobe.
Oh Oracle, can you see back to when we were but babes?
If we, tabula rasa, were anything but blank slates?
Nothing to fear but fear itself, so conquer it and see.
You'll need some paper and a pen to write down this
story.
But even then, you know it well, the story doesn't start.
Not with blood or love or tears, but only memory rot.
The ghosts of what you once had, that you wanted, are
all gone.
And yet you've resurrected them and, jaded, they live on.
Some foreign land, deep in that dome, these shadowed
mirrors move.
Known by one, explored by none, existing only to soothe.
So wander til you die, be it on sea or ice or sand.
The scientists know nothing of this unnamed barren
land.

Eiseley, Loren. *The Unexpected Universe*. Harcourt Brace & Company, 1964.

Hello Ghost Tornado

If you're a tornado, so am I. Smaller, but still capable of destruction. I had to survive somehow.

How could you?

The grief measures about the same, from zero to infinity all at once, wouldn't you say?

I don't understand.

What inheritance have I except the stain of mistakes, yours and mine, all tangled together?

I've suffered.

I've come anyway to try and find you somewhere in these mountains of sorrow we've both hid in all these years.

I need to know.

If you're anything like regret, I'm your ghost materialized. Will you confront me?

Hello.

A Prayer

Universe without end,
I sit on a rock in the heat on a dying planet,
waiting for the sun to burst and swallow us whole.

But she won't, not yet,
and so, while I wait, I soak up her power so that
perhaps one day I, too, can burn everything in my path.

Amen.

A Ghost in Dallas

She calls me from her Ghost Kingdom.
And because I know she's so cozy there,
I walk in the door and settle in.

I never know when my phone will ring,
but so far, I've been able to take her calls
and hear the despair in her voice.

"I want to live with you."

The ghosts that haunt her are timeless.
We've missed thirty-two years and don't have much time
left.

"Come get me."

I radiate love when I speak to her; I hope she feels it.
It's all I have left to give.
That and the playful fantasy of what we both wish could
be.

"I'll be there soon."

Mother Daughter Silence

When I look at her, I see a past I'll never know.
When she looks at me, she sees a future she'll never have.
Neither of us will get what we want so we sit in the
courtyard together in silence.

Her true feelings are artfully hidden from me, despite
the dementia.
My true feelings don't matter to a dying woman who
wants to believe she made the right choice.
Neither of us can speak the truth so we sit in the
courtyard together in silence.

The silence is all we have.

For Remembering

The leaves were yellow,
and the wind was fierce.
my hair, unwashed,
tangled while I stood outside
on my own march to the end.
I should have told you last time,
but I didn't.
A cold day in November
came for the last time today.
How did I sleep under that
half moon last night
with you so far away?
The leaves were yellow,
and the wind was fierce.
the day I got that call.

Paper Birds

When you took your last breath,
I was dreaming.
Paper birds flew about our heads,
stuffed with the secrets of our lives.
Burn them, burn them, we cackled,
and with our fingertips, we set them aflame.
I stood among the charred remains,
your nurse on the other side of the phone.
When you took your last breath,
was I dreaming?

Goodbye Mom

I'm sorry I didn't send you a vape in the mail.
I'm sorry I couldn't answer all of your calls.
I'm sorry I wasn't there with you.

I was going to tell you I was mad.
I was going to tell you that it hurt.
And then I was going to forgive you.

But that last part, it's more for me.
And I will.

And when I do drop these burdens,
I will go to war for families like ours.
You deserved help, support, and care.

Goodbye mom, I hope you rest in peace.

Divorce and Death

My mother dying reminds me of my world lit professor's reaction to my divorce. I had her for the first time in the fall about three months after the paperwork had been finalized by a judge.

"Oh, I'm okay, that was in May," I told her, brushing it off.
"You're not okay, it just happened," she told me, her face full of shock.

She was right, though, and it took me the next couple of years before I'd worked through enough of it to pass as a somewhat healed human.

I can see it more clearly now, the mask I hold up when I know that others are unprepared or unwilling to sit with me in my grief. I can also see the path ahead of me, rockier than ever, another few years of wandering before I can find my way again.

Broken Locket

It snapped when I pulled it
and I snapped like a bullet;
This bullshit breaks me,
makes my heart achy.

A rose on a locket
and you fucking forgot it.
Now there's nothing left,
now you've fucking left.

So the chain is broken,
and I'm fucking chokin'.
'Cause there's nothing here
except for these dry tears.

But I'll treasure the trash
with you in a cask.
Hey, aren't we quite the pair?
I'm the heir of no spare.

Haunted Etymology

Fantastic.

A phantom.

A fantasy.

These are the ghosts we made, you and me.

A specter.

A haunt.

An apparition.

Rise from the past, our superstitions.

Phantasm.

Fiction.

Delusion of mind.

Our pain made visible, regrets intertwined.

Regret

Regret is a ghost that kisses me in the morning.

I should have.

Regret is a ghost that looks at me in the mirror.

I could have.

Regret is a ghost that sits with me in my car.

I would have.

Regret is the ghost of a moment I might have loved.

But I didn't.

<u>Change</u>

The last goodbye, an unknown sorrow.

Our last hug, a welcome joy.

Just us girls, no need for talk of boys.

Silver in her hair and a gold locket

hanging around my neck.

We share one last secret between us.

I'll never tell, and anyway, words won't do it justice.

So, I fold these black wings inside of myself

and wait to hear her laugh

the next time a crow caws.

Counting Crows. "A Murder of One." *August and Everything After*, Geffen, 1993. .

"One for Sorrow (nursery rhyme)." *Wikipedia, The Free Encyclopedia*, Wikimedia Foundation, 9 Jan.2024. Accessed 18 Jan. 202

Appreciation

In the words of Snoop Dog, I would first like to thank me for believing in me. This project was halfheartedly in the works during the short time I was in reunion with my mother, but when she passed, it became my top priority. I am so thankful to all of those close to me who willingly walked beside me through some of the hardest months of my life and cheered me on as I put together this work of art. I heal in piles of papers that need organizing, that's for sure.

First, thank you to Emery. Without you, I would have much less reason to document the goings-on of my life. I hope that, as you continue to grow, you will better understand the importance of the words that I leave to you. Also, thank you for being so excited about this project. Your eagerness to make me cover art once I told you about my plans for a poetry book melted my heart. I'm so lucky to have you around. It is such a blessing to have an artist in the family.

Thank you to my Aunt Bev who was the first person to review this manuscript and the only one I really needed to hear say that it was okay to send this out into the world. I am so happy to be your niece.

Many thanks to my favorite artist in the world, Theo Underhill, who has continually taken my half-baked ideas and made them into beautiful art to accompany my words. Your talent continues to astound me.

I'd also like to extend a special thanks to the people who took the time to review various drafts of this collection and offer their feedback. It really takes a village and I'm so thankful for your help. Thank you to: Marci Purcell, Hannah Andrews, Beth Headrick, Akara Skye, Michael Hilton, and Savannah Simmons. Sparkly special thanks to Daniel Stefanelli who helped me with my weird citations, too.

Thank you to everyone who took the time to support me by pre-ordering this book: Andie Coston, Beth Headrick, Bethany Weston, Bev Eston, Daniel Stefanelli, Dawn Yip, Dianne Sonnenberg, Ellen Guerrero, Erik Jones, Glen & Joan Quist, G Busl, Hannah Andrews, Janet Slaughter, Jenny Russell, Kelsey Smith, Kim Newton, Kyle Vernor, Linda Ball, Lindsay Livingston, Marci Purcell, Marci Shrull, Megan Diaz, Michelle Perry, Michelle Simmons (both of you!), Paula Ferguson, Sanlyn Ferguson, Shota & Ria Yamaguchi, Theodore Underhill, Tracy Ramacher, and the anonymous donors. Your excitement for this project warmed my heart and made this publication possible.

And last, but certainly not least, I'd like to thank all of those in the adoption community who continue to amplify adoptee voices, educate people on the complexities of adoption, fight for open records, and everything else you do to push the needle forward. I am inspired by you and honored to be a part of a collective group of people so determined to change things for the better.

Shannon Quist (she/her) is the author of *Rose's Locket* and a board member for Adoption Knowledge Affiliates. She currently haunts her bespoke ghost kingdom and spends her days writing in practically every genre. She hopes to die someday in a library of her own words.

Calling All Ghost Kingdom Hunters!

In Betty Jean Lifton's 1994 book, *Journey of the Adopted Self: A Quest for Wholeness*, she explained that the Ghost Kingdom is a "psychic reality" where what-if projections of lost or wished-for persons (often conceptualized as ghosts) reside. In other words, a ghost kingdom is a fantasy that people in the adoption constellation engage in to imagine their lost family members due to family separation. For example, when I was a child, I used to daydream that my birthmother would come rescue me on her motorcycle. You can learn more about ghost kingdoms at www.shannonquist.com if you need additional information.

Your task is to locate these fantasies in the wild and report them to me. Submissions will be accepted via email to wordnoodlepress@gmail.com. Please include where you found the ghost kingdom, your explanation for why it is a ghost kingdom, and your mailing address. Successful submissions will earn you a bookmark declaring you a "Certified Ghost Kingdom Hunter."

P.S. Book reviews will also earn you a bookmark. Send me a screenshot of your posted review and your mailing address via an email to wordnoodlepress@gmail.com to receive your bookmark.

www.ingramcontent.com/pod-product-compliance
Lightning Source LLC
Chambersburg PA
CBHW060342130626
46553CB00003B/1079

* 9 7 9 8 2 1 8 3 9 6 4 0 4 *